Mercer Mayer

Jennifer Strand

abdopublishing.com

Published by Abdo Zoom™, PO Box 398166, Minneapolis, Minnesota 55439. Copyright © 2017 by Abdo Consulting Group, Inc. International copyrights reserved in all countries. No part of this book may be reproduced in any form without written permission from the publisher. Abdo Zoom™ is a trademark and logo of Abdo Consulting Group, Inc.

Printed in the United States of America, North Mankato, Minnesota
062016
092016

Cover Photo: Doug Oudekerk
Interior Photos: Doug Oudekerk, 1, 18; Mercer Mayer, 5; Adam Springer/iStockphoto, 6–7; hanayama/Shutterstock Images, 7; iStockphoto, 8–9, 10; Shutterstock Images, 11; Steve Debenport/iStockphoto, 12; Wavebreakmedia/iStockphoto, 13; Monkey Business Images/Shutterstock Images, 14; Wong Sze Yuen/Shutterstock Images, 15; Donald Erickson/iStockphoto, 17; Christopher Futcher/iStockphoto, 19

Editor: Emily Temple
Series Designer: Madeline Berger
Art Direction: Dorothy Toth

Publisher's Cataloging-in-Publication Data
Names: Strand, Jennifer, author.
Title: Mercer Mayer / by Jennifer Strand.
Description: Minneapolis, MN : Abdo Zoom, [2017] | Series: Amazing authors |
    Includes bibliographical references and index.
Identifiers: LCCN 2016941360 | ISBN 9781680792171 (lib. bdg.) |
    ISBN 9781680793857 (ebook) | 9781680794748 (Read-to-me ebook)
Subjects: LCSH: Mayer, Mercer, 1943-- Juvenile literature. | Authors, American--
    20th century--Biography--Juvenile literature. | Children's stories--
    Authorship--Juvenile literature.
Classification: DDC 813/.54 [B]--dc23
LC record available at http://lccn.loc.gov/2016941360

Table of Contents

Introduction

Mercer Mayer writes children's books. He is also an **illustrator**. He has made more than 300 books.

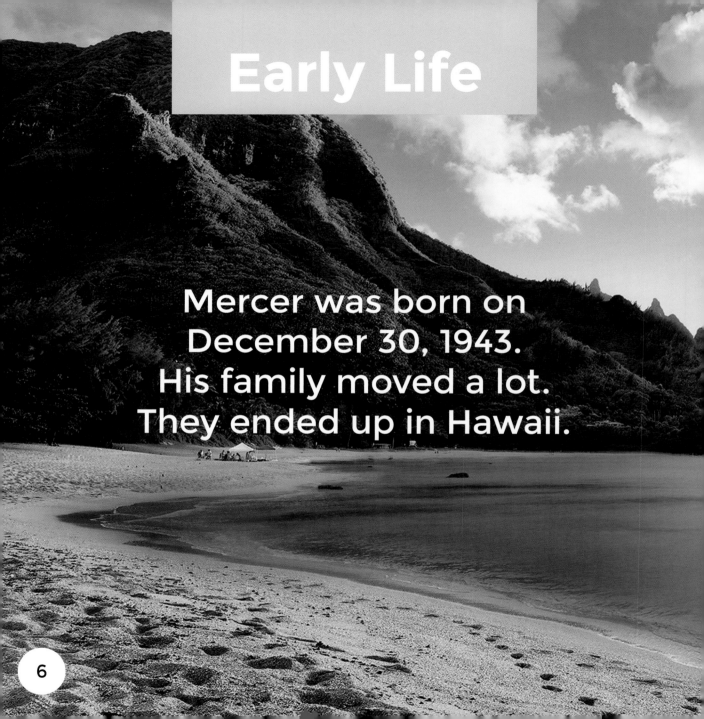

Early Life

Mercer was born on December 30, 1943. His family moved a lot. They ended up in Hawaii.

Mercer studied at an
arts school. He decided
to become an illustrator.

Rise to Fame

In 1964 Mayer moved to New York. He worked on his **technique**.

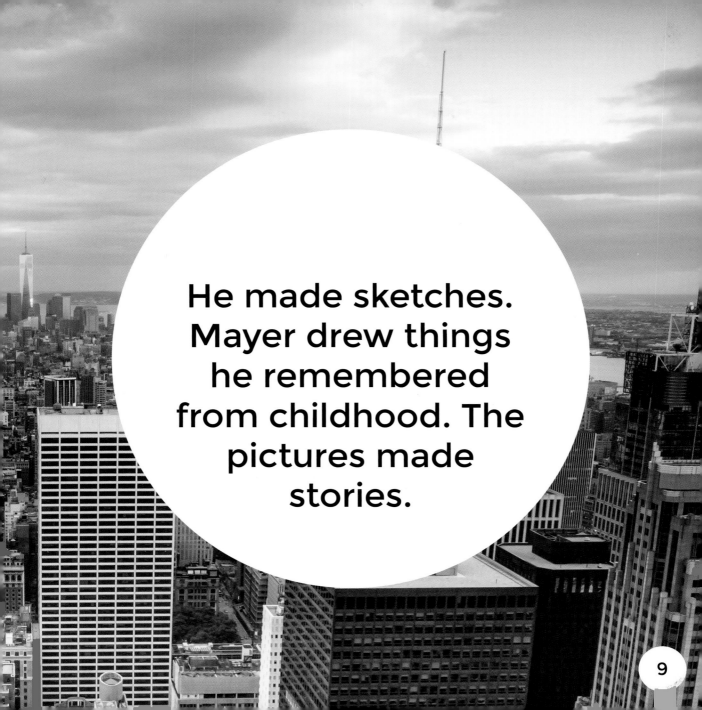

He made sketches. Mayer drew things he remembered from childhood. The pictures made stories.

Mayer's first book was
A Boy, A Dog, and A Frog.
It showed their adventures.

There were no words.
Pictures told the story.

Career

Mayer wrote more books. They were **popular**.

They were about things kids understood. He wrote about being scared or angry.

Mayer wrote about a funny animal.
It was called *Little Critter*.

Mayer wrote more books about Little Critter. They were a **series**.

At first Mayer made his
illustrations with ink.
Later he used a computer.

Mayer still writes
and illustrates books.

Children enjoy his **characters**.
They learn from them, too.

Mercer Mayer

Born: December 30, 1943

Birthplace: Little Rock, Arkansas

Known For: Mayer is a children's book author and illustrator. He created the *Little Critter* series.

1943: Mercer Mayer is born on December 30.

1967: *A Boy, a Dog, and a Frog* is published.

1968: Mayer publishes *There's a Nightmare in My Closet*.

1975: The first *Little Critter* book is published.

1998: Mayer begins using his computer to illustrate.

2007: Mayer creates artwork for the National Book Festival.

Glossary

characters - people in a story.

illustrator - an artist who creates pictures that help tell a story. The pictures are called illustrations.

popular - liked or enjoyed by many people.

series - a group of books or movies about the same characters.

technique - the skills that help a person do a job or task well.

Booklinks

For more information
on **Mercer Mayer**, please visit
booklinks.abdopublishing.com

Z∞m™ In on Biographies!

Learn even more with the Abdo Zoom
Biographies database. Check out
abdozoom.com for more information.

Index